Meditative Metamorphosis: A Poetic Manifestation

Deja Craft

BookLeaf Publishing

India | USA | UK

Presentation by *BookLeaf Publishing*

Web: www.bookleafpub.com

E-mail: info@bookleafpub.com

ISBN: 9789363301108

First edition 2024

Seeds of Change

In the quiet of the dawn, I lie
A humble seed beneath the sky
With dreams of life so vibrant and bright
As I inch along, I seek the light
In every step, I find my place
With poise and patience, moving at my own
pace
For though I'm small, my heart is strong
In this world, I do belong
In the soil, where roots are deep
I plant my hopes and dreams to keep
With every leaf, with every breath
I conquer fear, I conquer death
In this stage, I start to grow
A journey long, a path I know
For I am more than what I seem
A mere soul as a seed, with big dreams

Journey of the Small

Beneath the sun, I make my way
With gratitude, I greet the day
With every thought, a story spun
Of battles fought, of victories won
I weave my strength in silken threads
In dreams where future hopes are fed
A humble start, a seed of might
I strive and strive, to reach the distant light
The world is vast, yet here I stand
A tiny soul, a future unplanned
In every inch, in every move
I find my way, I find my groove
Through the challenges, through wind and rain
I grow through joy, I grow through pain
In this moment, I lay the ground
For wings that soon will lift me, safe and sound

Hidden Strength

In the shadows where the sunlight gleams
I nurture my quiet, hidden dreams
With growing confidence and a patient heart
I know each day brings a new start
The earth beneath, the sky above
Surround me with such gentle love
In every breath, I find my way
Through my silent, hidden strength
Each road I travel, each ladder I climb
Reminds me of the passing time
And in this state, I lay my base
A future bright, a destined place
Though small in form, my spirit grows
Through all life's highs, through all its lows
And in the quiet, I prepare
For wings that soon will lift me there

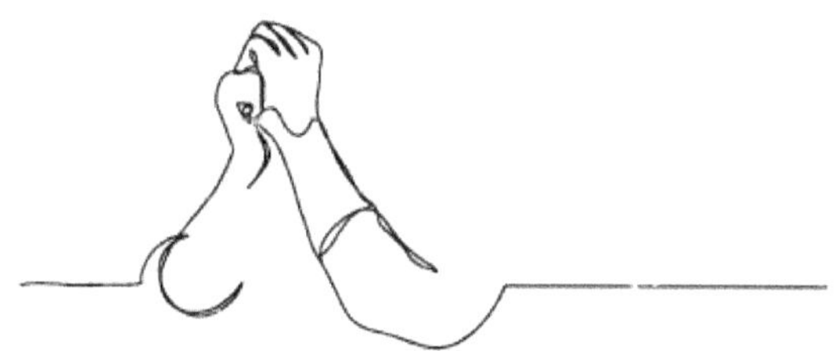

Path of Dreams

With every step, a promise kept
A path of dreams where hope has slept
In a shy humble guise
I see the world through patient eyes
In Earth's embrace, I find the way
Through sunlit beams and shades of gray
I weave my story, thread by thread
In whispers soft, in words unsaid
The journey long, the path unknown
Yet in my heart, the seeds are sown
For every inch, for every try
I reach for stars, I touch the sky
Here I am, I learn to see
The strength that lies inside of me
With perseverance, grace, and might
I inch my way towards the light

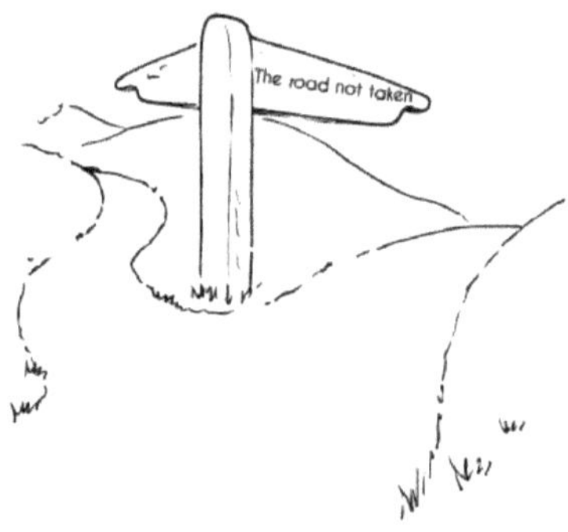

The Soil of Patience

In the quiet dawn of dreams,
A seed begins its silent scream
Within the earth, deep and unseen
A future bright, yet still so dark it seems
Patience is the soil's embrace
Nurturing with gentle grace
Through the tender rain, my roots sustain
Growth is slow, yet ever so sure
Through the darkness, strength will endure
Whispers of potential might
Guide me through the longest nights
In the soil of patience, my roots grow deep
Each challenge faced, my dreams I still keep

Rise unbound

Perseverance in the small
Each step I rise, despite the falls
In silent work, the strength I find
To weave the threads of grand design
My journey long, the path unsure
Yet faith within will help endure
In every trial, lessons learned
A spark of hope, brightly burned
In every inch, my strength is found
With every fall, I rise unbound

The Promise of Tomorrow

In the heart of stillness grows
A promise of what tomorrow holds
With a patient heart and steady mind
The wings of change, seek to find
Believing in the dawn's first light
That ushers the wings for which it fights
Perseverance is its song
A melody both pure and strong
In every heartbeat, whispers say
Success will come with each new day
With a patient heart and steady mind
The life I dream, will soon be mine

The Embrace

In the depths of challenge, I reside
Just like a caterpillar, with beauty inside
Through the trials and the strife
I find the will to embrace this life
With every inch, I push ahead
Through the doubts that cloud my head
I stay strong, my spirit high
Knowing that, someday I`ll fly
In every challenge, I find my strength
My desires will come at any length

The Power Within

Amid the trials, I remain
A dancing soul in the rain
Each drop a test, each step a stride
With inner strength, I will abide
Through tough times, I hold on tight
A beacon glowing in the night
With faith in what may lie ahead
My path is clear, all doubts are dead
In tough times, my strength will shine
My wishes are clear, they will be mine

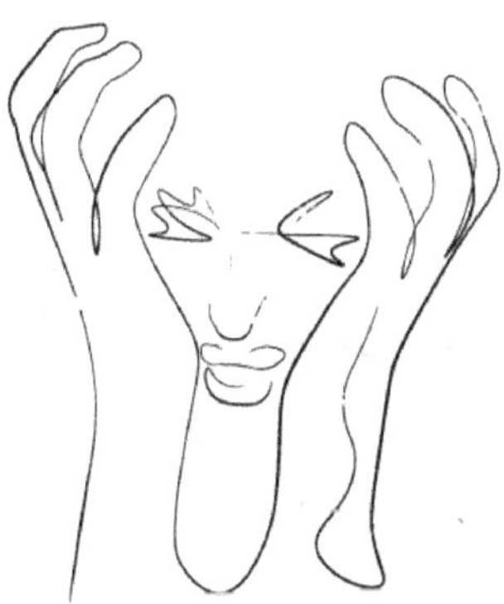

The Journey

In the shadow of the storm
A warrior's strength is born
Through the darkest of nights, I tread
With hope and courage, fully fed
I rise above, with a heart so strong
Knowing I will find where I belong
Through every struggle, every tear
My dreams draw closer, ever near
In resilience, my dreams take flight
With strength and hope, I find my light

The Embrace of Stillness

Subdued in the earth's quiet fold
An element of stillness, brave and bold
Wrapped in peace, my imagination takes flight
Dreams I have, of a beautiful life

Patience is the heart's favorite song
A lullaby so pure and strong
In the calm, my mind finds rest
Preparing for this journey's quest
In stillness, I find my peace
In patience, all my worries cease

The Dreamers Key

Within my mind, the world is still
A sanctuary, for the dreamer's will
Here, dreams are whispered, hopes renewed
In tranquil silence, strength is brewed

My meditations are the sacred key
Unlocking realms of what can be
I release my wants, I let them flow
To a higher power, I let them go
In meditation, my heart finds light
Releasing desires, to the powers of light

The Patience of Becoming

Encased in threads of time and grace
My thoughts hold a sacred space
Where transformation gently brews
And future paths my soul pursues

Patience guides this quiet phase
A beacon through the misty haze
In surrender, my dreams align
With forces greater, more divine
With patience, I transform and grow
to higher realms, my thoughts may go

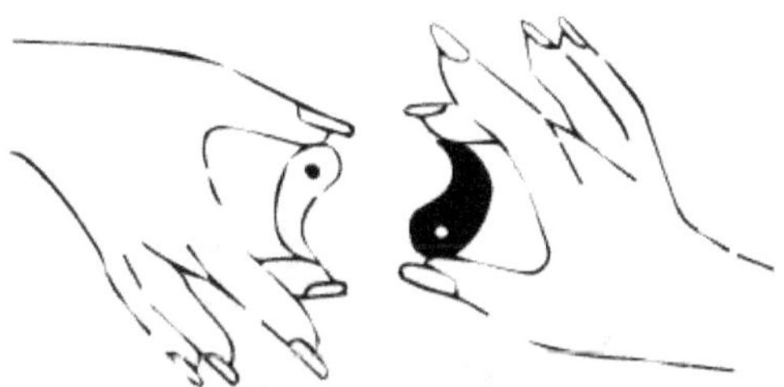

Meditative Dreams

Wrapped in stillness, calm and deep
My soul whispers dreams to keep
In silent change, the soul prepares
For the life ahead, as it dares

Peaceful moments, slow and true
Guide my heart to skies of blue
Meditation leads the way
To brighter nights and clearer days
In the stillness, I find my way
With strength and wit, come what may

The Promise Within

Within the earth's tender hold
Lies the promise of the bold
With positive thoughts and a patient heart
The old end, a brand-new start

I set my wishes on the breeze
Let them float with gentle ease
To the universe, I release my dreams
Trusting in life's unfolding schemes
With trust, my dreams take flight
With belief, I manifest my dream life

The Inner Sanctuary

My inner cocoon, a sacred space
Where my heart finds gentle grace
Meditation soothes my mind
In this refuge, strength I find

Patience is the guiding star
Leading us to who we are
Releasing wants, our spirits soar
To higher realms, forevermore
With perseverance, my dreams fly
To higher realms, beyond the sky

The Peaceful Pause

In the circle of life, we pause and wait
For life's grand plan to resonate
In solitude, dreams begin to weave
A tapestry of what I believe

Meditation clears the way
For the dawn of a brighter day
Release my wants, and let them be
Out into the universe, I set them free
In stillness, I find my peace
With trust, my worries cease

Embrace of Patience

Within the cocoon, time stands still
A gentle pause, a quiet thrill
Patience wraps its soothing arms
Shielding from the world's alarms
In this space, the heart finds peace
A time for dreams to grow, increase
With faith in what the future brings
In stillness, strength begins to sing
With patience, my strength will grow
With time, my dreams will surely show

Guided by Light

In my cocoon, a soft glow shines
A beacon through the tangled vines
Guidance whispers in the dark
Igniting the smallest spark
With every breath, a step is made
Towards my dreams that won't fade
Trust in the path, trust in the light
In the cocoon, your goals take flight
With guidance, my path is clear
With trust, my goals will draw near

Knowing Within

In this phase, the heart knows well
That in this pause, success begins to swell
A sacred space, a quiet bloom
Where goals are nurtured in the gloom
Patience holds the dreams so tight
Perseverance leads me through the darkest
nights
With every moment, trust and know
Staying positive makes my desires glow

Wings of Fulfillment

In the dawn when dreams come true
The butterfly, in skies so blue
Flutters with a heart so light
In the warmth of morning's light

Manifested wishes, bright and clear
In its flight, there is no fear
Prosperity in every wing
Beauty in the song it sings
With wings of light, my wishes take flight
My thoughts manifest my dreams overnight

The Dance of Grace

With delicate wings, they dance so high
A testament to wishes that fly
Through fields of gold and skies of blue
The manifested butterfly, a dream come true

In every flutter, beauty is found
In every moment, dreams unbound
My wishes granted, life embraced
In the sunlight, gently traced
In every dance, my wants align
With grace and beauty, they are mine

The Bloom of Abundance

A butterfly, in colors hued
A symbol of abundance vast
In every moment, joy is cast

Prosperity in petals bright
In every flower, pure delight
Wishes granted, my heart's desires
With every manifestation, my soul climbs higher
In abundance, I find my way
With every wish, comes a brighter day

Becoming

The joy of becoming, the heart sings
Dreams manifested wishes clear
In the gentle breeze, there is nothing to fear

Beauty flows in every turn
For abundance, the heart does yearn
With love and light, the path is shown
In this flight, my soul has grown
With every twist and turn, my strength shows
With divine love, my spirit grows

The Light of Dreams

In the sunlight, my dreams take form
In the night, the divine guides my path, safe and
warm
Wishes granted, life anew
With every color, with every hue

Abundance blows in the gentle breeze
With every flutter, my heart is at ease
Beauty is found in the simplest things
In every beat, my soul sings
In the sunlight's glow, my dreams are seen
In every hue, a life beyond my wildest dreams

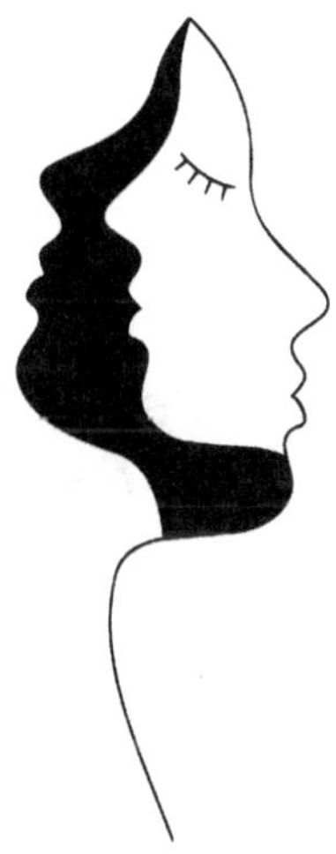

The Journey of Light

From earth to sky, the journey is made
In butterfly wings, dreams cascade
My wishes have been granted, to my heart's
delight
With every manifestation, my dreams soar to
new heights

Gratitude in every glance
I see the beauty in life's dance
Manifested dreams, so pure and true
In every wingbeat, life feels anew
In every glance, success is near
In every dance, my dreams appear

The Symphony of Success

In the symphony of success so bright
This butterfly finds pure delight
My desires fulfilled, wishes grant
In every step, a promised land

Abundance in colors bold
In every story, life unfolds
Beauty in the dreams achieved
With each moment, my heart is relieved
In every step, success I see
In every attempt, prosperity

The Triumph in Transformation

In the dance of sunlight's glow
A butterfly dreams in tow
Fulfilled wishes, goals achieved
The journey's worth, now firmly believed
Wings spread wide, heart full of grace
I have achieved my goals, no matter the pace
Dreams fulfilled, pure and bright
A testament to my inner might
In transformation, my dreams arise
No matter the challenge, I survive

The Beauty of Fulfillment

From the caterpillar's toil, wings unfold
A butterfly emerges, with stories untold
Each wish fulfilled, each goal embraced
The journey etched in time and space
Beauty in the flight so free
A life well-lived, a destiny
Every step, a path well-tread
Worth it all, the dreams ahead
With fulfillment, my spirit sings
With every step, I follow my dreams

The Joy of Arrival

In the skies, my wishes soar
With dreams accomplished, longing no more
The journey long, but worth the flight
In every struggle, newfound light
Fulfilled wishes, to my heart's delight
My life transformed, pure and bright
In every flutter, joy is found
In every moment, dreams unbound
In arrival, my dreams align
Every journey, worth the climb